Herbs for Fun

ELIZABETH WALKER

Herbs for Fun

Illustrated by
LINDA DIGGINS

Darton, Longman and Todd

First Published in Great Britain in 1977
by Darton, Longman and Todd Ltd
85 Gloucester Road, London SW7 4SU

ISBN 0 232 51368 6

Cover by Anthony Moore

Printed and bound in Great Britain by
Cox & Wyman Ltd, London, Reading and Fakenham

Contents

Introduction

A picture of a country house stillroom in Elizabethan times is certainly charming and nostalgic but it is also one of quite compelling topical interest. Now that we are all using herbs once again in so many ways, and are increasingly aware of the subtle fragrance and flavours they yield, and of their powers and pleasures, the time seems particularly right for a return to the 'stillroom', even if it is only a corner of the kitchen or the cupboard under the stairs, as few people will have enough space to devote a whole room in the house to this purpose. Your stillroom could be made in a garden shed or an attic; it should be dry and not subject to extremes of heat or cold – a really dry cellar, with its temperate atmosphere, can be ideal. But even a large old wardrobe will do.

Old stillroom books, which gradually superseded the Herbals of the fifteenth and sixteenth century, are fortunately still to be found in libraries and museums – and can indeed sometimes be picked up in bundles of books in salerooms and in junkshops. These give us all sorts of wonderful glimpses of the housewife's treasury of herbs and the way she used them in her domestic life, especially in the making of charming personal presents and of small embellishments to the home. The stillroom was away from the bustle of the kitchen and larders, the laundry room and the servants' hall, and was usually the domain of the mistress of the house, her friends, her daughters and, in the larger house, the numerous female relatives and connections who would be living there. There they would make up toilet vinegar, hair rinses, soap balls, sweet-bags for chests and linen presses, little herb bags to scatter in the rooms and drawers, herb candles and fragrant blends of pot-pourri. The latter were essential to dispel the mustiness of the rooms, both in large and small houses – for these lacked any sort of protection against the damp, and were often ill lit and ill ventilated. From early times beautifully worked little cushions and pillows containing mixtures of herbs and other such scented delights, flowers and spices were made from 'receipts' which would be handed down or exchanged as favourite cooking recipes or knitting patterns are today. Later, particularly in the Victorian age, when all sorts of pastimes became fashionable among cultured young ladies, flowers would be pressed for the making of gift cards and bookmarks and for collecting for the scrap book – and for pressing among the pictures and scraps which decorated the draught screens of the day.

Decoctions and distillations of rose petals, lavender flowers, elder flowers, vervain and a score of others would be made in the old fashioned stillroom, and bunches of herbs would be hanging drying from the ceiling – not only the familiar mint, parsley, sage and rosemary, for from the hedges and fields there would be bunches of hay-scented woodruff – for strewing and to combat fleas; heady meadow-sweet; pungent tansy; soapwort for washday; antiseptic thyme; comfrey for many ills; rosehips and limeflowers for teas; chamomile for comfort and valerian for sleep. On the shelves would be books of herbal remedies and simples, recipes for lotions and creams, scales, measures, pestle and mortar, scissors, needles and thread, bowls and pans for the mixing of pot-pourri and concoctions for spice bags and scented pillows. It would be a sweet smelling room, and as so many herb

'And on the shelf would be the pestle and mortar . . .'

scents are soothing, curative and refreshing, I can imagine how sometimes the tired and harassed lady of the house would like to slip away to work among the herbs appreciatively sniffing lavender, the rosemary and the bay leaves.

Few of us today can spare room for such a romantic scene, nor time for such brewing and strewing, tending and blending, but in this short book I would like to encourage the idea of a modified stillroom store from which could stem all sorts of delightful pastimes and activities. In this day of 'collecting' mania, I can think of many practical and interesting collections to be started as a basis for a stillroom of the second Elizabethan era. Pestles and mortars, herb prints, old stillroom books and herbals – and present day ones too (see bibliography) old pomanders, toilet water bottles, scent bottles, pot-pourri containers, measures, then rare spices, oils. . . . But whether collections are to be initiated or not, there are a few simple items that it would be convenient to get together if some of the ideas in this book are to be explored – ideas which it is hoped will lead to individual experiments and creations, for I do not aim to set out rules and patterns. For your stillroom you will need a good strong table or shelf with some sort of waterproof top, and plenty of shelf space for materials and equipment. A measuring jug, marked in cubic centimetres, pints and grams and/or ounces – and, as you never know how recipes which you like will be measured, a metric conversion table is an asset. Large bowls, a good strong pestle and mortar (second-hand probably, but *heavy*), a fine sieve, a funnel, a large wooden spoon – one of those huge hand carved trouble-stirrers is good – a cloth or kitchen paper rolls for mopping up scent oils and wiping out oily jugs, a muslin nose protector (if you are apt to be sensitive to fine dust), and a pencil and notebook, sewing materials, some tight lidded jars and a shelf for books complete your basic store. Those are merely tools; the books, the coloured petals, the aromatic leaves, the herbs and spices, the essential oils, the fabrics, the fun of collecting these together comes next.

I

Pot-pourri

Making pot-pourri at home is a pursuit which most delightfully titillates both eye and nose. It leads one into exciting excursions into the past in search of old 'receipts', and to experiments with fragrance and colour. It is a pity to feel slavishly obliged to follow exactly the various classic recipes that make such fascinating reading and indeed it is frequently impossible to do so. The adventurous cook does not obey exactly the dictates of Mrs Beeton – or not for long. In fact, as with pot-pourri, some of her ingredients may prove difficult or impossible to find, and many may be too expensive. I tend to compare the blending of pot-pourri with cooking because it can be as creative, as satisfying and as individual, appealing to the senses of smell and colour as cooking does to taste and colour, but giving, I may add, a pleasure which will last very much longer than a gourmet dinner.

It is better, then, to start with a simple form of one of the many classic recipes – a selection of which I give – but feel encouraged to add, or substitute, from the stock in your garden, in the hedgerows and fields, from the spices in your kitchen, and from the growing collection of dried flowers, petals and leaves which you have been accumulating in your stillroom cupboard and shelves, together with oils and herbs you have purchased. Keep a record of your blends, particularly those that please you – it is extraordinarily difficult to re-create a veritable symphony of aroma that is your great pride if you have not noted the inspired last minute addition of a sprinkle of allspice or a drop of bergamot oil which made all the difference. I think it is helpful and interesting to write down as many of your efforts as please you, or as may form the basis for future experiments. Philippa Back's book in this series (*Profitable Herbs*) gives detailed and expert advice on growing, harvesting and drying herbs, not only in gardens but also in boxes and tubs and in the house, and there are countless books on the cultivation of aromatic flowers. Therefore, I want to concentrate on the next stage, not only for those with gardens, but for anyone who can acquire petals, herbs, leaves by any means – country walks, buying from herbalists, begging from neighbours with gardens and even collecting the petals from their own vases about the house – but *before* they are in a condition only for the dustbin.

By the time the hobby of pot-pourri blending becomes addictive (and it does), you will have become increasingly acquisitive – flower heads and leaves will have been collected during the spring and summer and dried awaiting blending, jars will contain dried herbs; with these there will be oils and whole and ground spices bought at different times, pretty leaves and berries drying, citrus peel cut and dried awaiting mincing in the blender. The habit grows; in not too long a time you will acquire a veritable library of smells and a glorious palette of colours to use.

To summarise some of the points which have been extensively covered in the harvesting sections in previous books in the series – *Profitable Herbs* and *A Book of*

Aromatics by Roy Genders – ensure that only healthy blooms are used, picked when quite dry; never pick after rain, or when the dew is still upon the plants, and avoid humid days. Pick in the peak of condition, dry away from strong light, never in sunlight, which not only fades the colours but destroys the aromatic oils. An airy place is best – my own favourite is slatted shelves in the airing cupboard, or between newspaper under beds, suspended in net or in muslin bags in a drafty spot, spread in a garden shed if not too stuffy and humid, spread on muslin or net stretched like hammocks in the loft, or, if you are in a hurry, even in the slow oven of your cooker with the door slightly open. Alternatively, flowers and herbs may be suspended from hooks in bunches, heads down, in a warm airy kitchen or loft, or even better, in your stillroom where they will look charming while drying. Special drying racks can also be made by tacking muslin over prepared wooden frames; as a further step, these can be arranged like shelves in a tall frame. A special drying room can also be prepared, but these more sophisticated drying techniques need only be considered if you are planning to dry herbs and flowers on a large scale.

Drying may take from four to ten days according to the flower or herb and the humidity – they should be as crisp as cornflakes and should 'whisper' like dry leaves when you handle them. Keep some whole flower heads intact (those which have dried a good shape) and you can ensure a supply of these by drying some perfect flowers and perhaps a whole stem of a herb such as thyme or borage in a covering of silversand or silica gel, which can be sieved away and will leave you with a perfect specimen as used for dried flower arrangements. These greatly enhance the appearance of a presentation box or jar of pot-pourri if arranged judiciously on the surface.

Blending of dried pot-pourri should be done in the following order: put the petals, flowers, leaves and herbs in a large bowl, pan or crock; add first the fixative and stir well, turning over and over with the hand; this will help to retard the evaporation of the natural oils; then a mixture of spices, next any special subtleties you choose, and lastly, drop by drop, the fragrant oils or essences selected. Add spices and oils sparingly and gradually, so that you do not run the risk of killing the original fragrance instead of enhancing it. If making larger quantities of pot-pourri than given in the recipe, introduce one or two additional essences rather than increasing pro-rata the original oils, which may otherwise become rather overpowering and unsubtle.

Choose and use a variety of colours and scents – the following list may remind you of some of the many ingredients you already have in the garden or kitchen; oils can be purchased from various suppliers, some of which are listed at the end of this book.

AROMATIC FLOWERS

Roses – many varieties of differing shades and scents; lavender, violets, pinks, jasmine, orange-blossom, lilac, stocks, wallflowers, peony, honeysuckle, mignonette, limeflower, heliotrope, Roman chamomile.

LEAVES

Geranium, lemon verbena, lemon balm, bay, box, sweet myrtle, patchouli, eucalyptus.

FLOWERS FOR COLOUR

Larkspur, delphinium, cornflower, marigold, nasturtium, candytuft, pansies, borage, bergamot, anchusa, hydrangea, salvia, forget-me-not, zinnias and the petals of all 'daisy-shaped' flowers.

HERBS

Basil, marjoram and rosemary; thyme, lovage and sage; tarragon, sweet cicely and dill; mint (many varieties), spearmint and peppermint; meadowsweet, tansy and santolina; sweet wormwood, woodruff and southernwood.

FIXATIVES

Orris root, vetiver, gum benzoin, calamus, costmary, sandalwood, Tonquin bean, myrrh, frankincense, patchouli.

SPICES

Allspice, anise, cardamon, coriander, caraway, cinnamon, cloves, mace, nutmeg, ginger.

OTHER ADDITIVES FOR SUBTLETY

Cedarwood or sandalwood chips or raspings; root of ginger or vetiver, crushed; lemon, lime, orange, tangerine or mandarine peel dried, broken, minced or pounded; vanilla pod, Tonquin bean, or cinnamon stick, broken; juniper berries, cloves or peppercorns, crushed.

OILS

Patchouli, musk, rose, rose geranium, tuberose, violet, vetiver, sandalwood, geranium, lemon verbena, ylang-ylang, bergamot, lavender, vanilla, myrtle, jasmine, heliotrope, lilac, carnation, marigold, clover, chamomile, meadowsweet, thyme, sweet pea, mandarine, narcissus, honeysuckle, mignonette, bay, rosemary, cinnamon, elderflower, cedarwood, pine, sweet orange, lemongrass, jonquil, wallflower, night scented stock, wistaria, larch, lily of the valley, limeflower.

Blended Pot-Pourri Oils
(*to be purchased*)

1: Floral and fresh
2: Spicy and woody
3: Lavender with green herbs

Two classic recipes suitable for adaptation are:

1 1 quart rose petals (and peony petals)
1 pint lemon verbena (and/or geranium leaves)
½ pint lavender flowers
½ pint rosemary leaves
1 tablespoon sweet marjoram (and/or lemon thyme)
1 tablespoon mixed crushed orris root and gum benzoin
1 tablespoon allspice and crushed cloves, to which add some grated nutmeg
10 drops rose oil
6 drops lemon verbena oil
3 drops rosemary oil, or 6 drops bergamot oil

2 1 quart rose petals
½ pint lavender flowers
1 tablespoon crushed orris root
1 teaspoonful anise seed
1 tablespoon broken cloves and cinnamon stick, crushed together
5 drops EACH of oils of jasmine, rose geranium, patchouli, rosemary

A Pungent sixteenth century recipe
(*coloured flowers may be added to this*):

1 pint leaves of peppermint, cut
1 pint thyme
1 pint lavender flowers
1 tablespoon crushed cloves and coriander
1 tablespoon well-crushed caraway seed
1 tablespoon crushed gum benzoin or orris root

Some wild herbs and flowers for pot-pourri – clover, ragwort, bindweed, wild rose and hedge parsley.

Basic green mix for pot-pourri

To 1 pint each of lemon verbena add ½ pint lavender, ¼ pint crushed rose petals and rose buds, 1 tablespoon each of thyme, basil and woodruff or southernwood or marigold, 1 dessertspoon of mixed spice; 1 dessertspoon powdered orris root. To this basic mixture a quart of rose, peony and other flower petals may be added from the garden and this quantity will require 10 drops of rose geranium oil or damask rose oil and 6 drops of lavender and green herbs oil or 3 drops of lemon verbena oil. As more flowers and leaves are added, stir in more crushed orris root, crushed cloves, bay leaf and a few drops of pot-pourri oil.

Once a basic mixture is established there are a number of imaginative variations which can be introduced and which will result in a really personal mixture. Suggestions are: add a few freshly dried mint leaves, a pinch of coriander powder, a piece of ginger root, pieces of dried orange peel (each with a clove stuck in it), a drop of vanilla essence, or cedarwood oil, a vanilla pod, or a fistful of marjoram. Orris root is preferred by me to gum benzoin as a fixative because it has such an interesting faded violet aroma of its own. It is most conveniently used in its powdered form but it is possible to hunt down suppliers of the whole rhizome. If this is grated the aroma is as different as that of freshly ground black pepper from the pre-packed variety but it is very hard work – somewhat worse than an old piece of Parmesan cheese.

My personal trick is to keep the piece of orris root in the bottom of the pot pourri bowl where it does its intended job to some extent and then, when passing fits of energy suggest, grate a little into the pot-pourri and put the piece back in the bottom of the bowl. I think it adds interest as well as aroma to the pot-pourri to have some whole spices and aromatics left in the bowl, such as a small stick of cinnamon, half a vanilla pod, a Tonquin bean or a little piece of ginger.

It is useful to keep in your stillroom, made up to about 4 oz. at a time:

Basic Spice mix for Pot-Pourri

½ oz. each cinnamon stick crushed to powder in mortar
broken cloves
powdered mace
gum benzoin (crushed)
powdered allspice, with a few whole crushed berries
whole coriander seeds (crushed)
powdered orris root

A pot-pourri of wild flowers and herbs

This can be most charming and unusual, with delicate colouring and aroma; but the utmost discretion should be exercised in collecting petals and leaves for this, remembering that many species of wild plants are endangered not only by land development, roadways, etc., but also by indiscriminate picking. It is safest to pick only on cultivated land or from hedgerows or fields which are to be scythed or ploughed, and then only in small quantities from plentiful crops. The same method of drying and blending applies as for garden mixtures, but thick heads such as clover, ragwort, burdock and wild chamomile need to be dried very slowly indeed, well separated from other plants; they especially need an airy place. Buttercup, poppy, wildrose, bindweed, toadflax and broom petals add colour, but will shrink greatly when drying; wildmint, woodruff, tansy and meadowsweet add aroma. The flowerets of the wild parsley family – cow parsley, fool's parsley, sweet cicely, caraway, hedge parsley, etc., give a pretty lacy effect on the top of your mixture, though the white will fade to brown; wild grasses pressed and laid flat over the blend look attractive. A delicate and grassy aroma seems more suitable for this pot-pourri, using more herbs, little or no spice and oils of meadowsweet, chamomile, thyme and myrtle.

This pot-pourri recipe was one used by Eleanour Sinclair Rohde and is included in her charming book of recipes.*

> 'To a large basin of dried sweet scented rose petals allow a handful of dried lavender flowers, rosemary, thyme, balm, sweet majoram, southernwood, sweet basil, clove carnations, sweet briar leaves, wild thyme, garden thyme, hyssop, philadelphus flowers, orange flowers, mint, sweet geranium leaves, verbena, a few bruised cloves, the dried and powdered rind of a lemon or orange, a teaspoonful of allspice, half an ounce of cinnamon and a good pinch of sandalwood.
>
> 'Gather and dry the flowers and leaves all through the season, adding any others according to one's fancy but keeping the proportion of a basin of rose petals to a large handful of all the other ingredients put together. Store in a jar with a lid, but the jar need not be airtight.'

Moist pot-pourri

All the pot-pourris so far described have been of the 'dry' variety, and this is by far the most usual method used today. Moist pot-pourri is quite another matter, not suitable for open bowls or sachets, but usually contained in pomanders or lidded jars. Such jars are opened on entering a room, and closed when the room is empty. As salt, and sometimes alcohol, is included in the recipes the

* *Rose Recipes from Olden Times*, Dover Books.

aroma tends to be particularly long-lasting, but it also takes much longer to make and to mature.

Moist pot-pourri is made in a large wide-necked crock or jar, into which are put alternate layers of scented flowers, rough salt (generally a mixture of common cooking salt and bay salt, but not iodised) and spices. These are pressed down and added to until the crock is full – this can be done over a period of time and as the flowers become available – and left to mature under an air-tight lid. Additives can include brandy, or cologne, or brown sugar. The following is an adaptation of a moist pot-pourri recipe from a stillroom book of 1834:

> 'Put into a large jar the following ingredients in layers, with bay salt strewed between the layers; rose petals and rose buds, orange blossom and jasmine about 2 gallons (a household bucket), an ounce each of sliced orris root, gum benzoin and storax, 10 drops of oil of musk, 2 ounces of angelica root, a handful of lavender flowers, half a handful of rosemary flowers and crushed bay leaf, three Seville oranges stuck as full of cloves as possible, dried in a cool oven and pounded in a mortar, half a handful of knotted marjoram and one handful of lemon balm. Cover all closely.'

The following is a simpler mixture, but it needs stirring daily for a month – a very pleasant task. Mix together first 1 oz. each of angelica root, gum benzoin, powdered cinnamon, powdered nutmeg, 2 oz. of powdered orris root, a few cloves and a very little grated lemon rind (free of pith); add 5 drops each of oil of bergamot and oil of musk. Put your dried rose and peony petals, and any scented flowers and leaves from the garden in inch deep layers in a large jar or crock; cover each layer with equal quantities of bay salt and the spice mixture you have already prepared. Fill only high enough in the crock to allow for stirring. This spicy and potent blend should be mature in a month to six weeks.

A sixteenth century recipe which is perfectly possible today, and is also simple if a little expensive, calls for 4 pints of rose petals and 1 pint of lavender flowers, 1 pint of verbena leaves and 1 pint of geranium leaves, to which are added 2 oz. each of kitchen salt, cloves, orris root, gum benzoin, allspice, brown sugar and a wineglassful of brandy. Stir daily. This should be fully matured, and very strong, in four weeks.

The 'dry' pot-pourri recipes would seem to lend themselves more readily to individual interpretation and adaptation, which is very much part of the fun of making one's own blends, and I was charmed to find a recipe in *The Complete Book of Herbs*, by Kay Sanecki, which well expresses this freedom and I cannot resist quoting it, with my thanks to her. She calls it 'The Cheat's Pot-pourri':

> 'Beg, steal, buy roses, carnations, sweet peas and lavender; gather from the fields meadowsweet, elderflowers and honeysuckle; dry the petals, and toss in a drop or two of oil of lavender, three crushed cloves, powdered cinnamon, borrowed from the neighbours, and two or three teaspoonfuls of the brandy known as "medicinal". Scatter in the box of pot-pourri sent by Aunt Agatha four Christmasses ago. Mix the ingredients together, add a drop or two of pot-pourri reviver and even one drop of a favourite floral perfume. Put into jars.'

I feel this sums up the whole subject of pot-pourri making very encouragingly, and helps to debunk the mystique which sometimes daunts the aspiring beginner.

2

Containers and holders

You can give your friend a small paper bag of parsley, thyme and a bay leaf and say to her 'Happy Birthday, I think these would be useful in the kitchen', and so they will be, and she will thank you and put them in her larder. Or you can go to your stillroom and choose a glass apothecary jar which you bought in a little junk shop in a country village five months ago and fill it with one of the blends mentioned in Chapter 5. Tie on to it a pretty tag listing the herbs used and it will seem a present which has been specially chosen with just that friend in mind and makes twice the impact. At no cost write two or three recipes which use the blend of herbs you are giving on the inside of your birthday card or add a paperback herb cooking book and it makes three times the gift.

In this way you have a ready made excuse for all the fun of collecting pots and jars and jugs and boxes all the year round, in all sorts of likely and unlikely places from country sale rooms to foreign souvenir shops and street markets. In writing this I feel I must alert the over enthusiastic collector; remember that you are looking for attractive but practical containers for your herb blends, pot-pourri, spices and so on, or you will be coming home

'Look for practical and attractive containers for your herb blends . . .'

with umbrella stands, chamber pots and other items which will be most unwelcome in your stillroom and may, alas, attract family ridicule. Some of the things I look out for include old oil and vinegar sets (minus the cumbersome holders), gravy boats, the little pots and jars that were included in Victorian dressing-table furniture and old apothecary jars and bottles. (Don't worry if they are lidless, you can buy from wine-makers' suppliers corks which can be cut to fit and can, if required, be judiciously 'antiqued' using materials to hand – cold tea makes a good stain if commercial dyes are not to hand, a rubbing of wax gives that antique 'feel'. But avoid dyes such as coffee, or finishes, which have a strong aroma of their own.) Old pomade pots, with lids or without and big Victorian mustard pots are among some of the things which may catch your eye and however many ideas one lists you will find something quite different which never before occurred to you as a possible herb container but will probably become your most prized item. When you are collecting, size, within reason, doesn't matter. A large old square decanter can be filled with a blend of herbs for the bath; a tiny antique thimble can be filled with expensive saffron. The liners, (usually of Bristol Blue glass) of silver mustard pots or sugar basins make superb gift containers for culinary aromatics.

Pot-pourri is rather a different matter. Consideration must be given to whether it is moist mixture requiring an air-tight lid, whether it is a particularly colourful one, whether you wish to display the maximum amount of petals or whether it is a highly aromatic blend of not particularly striking appearance that can go into an old pomander, an old pierced sugar sifter or an incense burner. If you wish to give a truly delicious present, a pot-pourri in a specially chosen open bowl is always preferred, if the receiver has not just the right bowl for the quantity you have given. If the filled bowl is to be presented or even posted two possible solutions are: (a) To cover the entire bowl and contents with colourful dress net, which can be bought from most shops which stock fabric, pull it very tightly to the base of the bowl, twist it round even more tightly and fasten with a wire twist, such as are given with plastic bags or sold for use in the garden. You can't find one? It will have to be a length of fine string, or Sellotape: (b) Simply seal the top with Cling Wrap, so modern and functional. It does absolutely nothing for the pot-pourri, but truth to tell is invaluable for many of the container ideas you may have.

It is hard to find original old pot-pourri vases and they are usually extremely expensive, as are also pomander pots with pierced lids and the rare pomander hinged boxes (similar to large vinaigrettes, also expensive rarities), and it is better therefore to keep one's eyes open for pretty bowls, and jars and pieces of pottery that can easily look as though they were purpose made when they are filled with fragrant pot-pourri, particularly if the colours seem to be in keeping. The unbroken remains of old tea sets and coffee sets are good containers – odd cups of the most beautiful hand painted china can be picked up very cheaply, and slight cracks won't matter.

The mellow glow of certain metals are highly complimentary to the soft colours of the old-fashioned pot-pourri, not only silver but copper, pewter and the often neglected Britannia metal make rare purchases to look for. Domestic items such as sugar bowls, coasters, creamers, tea caddies and tankards can often be found in street markets – the lesser known or the more out of the way if one is to avoid the high prices of famous markets like Portobello Road, in London. But remember that metal containers are only suitable for dry pot-pourri, not for culinary blends or for moist pot-pourri.

Wooden containers have an interesting affinity with aromatics, having indeed an aroma of their own. A pot-pourri containing sandalwood chips or cedar wood oil would be most suitable 'gift wrapped' in a cigar box or an old games or sewing box.

Now that so many people are collecting 'junk' and antiques of all kinds, you will have to look hard to find bargains. One source of supply may well be your own cupboards or those of friends and relatives – many people have unwanted china, glass and metal containers tucked away.

You can always aim to match the contents to the container – culinary blends in old kitchen ware and food receptacles, a pretty pot-pourri in a flowered bowl – or to create a deliberately contradictory effect: sometimes rather off-beat items such as old shaving-mugs and other bygones can be chosen to suit the taste or sense of humour of the recipient.

As well as antique containers, which may be hard to find if you have not already made a collection, many delightful objects are made today, and could be used or adapted. Simple glass bowls and tumblers are attractive; wooden bowls and jars; pottery bowls, mugs and containers. Crafts are now so popular that you may well have a friend experienced in potting or woodwork, from whom you could commission containers tailored to your needs – or learn how to do this for yourself! A simpler and cheaper idea is to put by the more attractive glass jars and glass bowls in which goods are bought and decorate these with glass paints.

3

Herb pillows and sachets

Blends for pillows and sachets

Perhaps the best known and oldest sleep inducer is the hop pillow. It is said that George III could not sleep without one; many people have been saying the same thing ever since. However there are many who just do not like the characteristic smell of hops, which can seem distinctly beery to the uninitiated, though this may surprise devotees of the classic hop pillow who find it a truly satisfying country smell. For others there are plenty of pleasant alternatives, although the smell of hops can be lessened by the addition of lemon verbena and mint. Lavender is not a suitable additive; the two smells make a rather sickly combination. If you are a true insomniac and find hops are not the answer, do experiment with other herb additives to improve the fragrance.

So effective are hops that a small sachet, say 6″ × 4″, which can be placed under the pillow is often enough – this is judged to be the most effective position, but they can be hung in a muslin dolly bag from the bedhead. Hops are particularly attractive, in lovely shades of greens, and lend themselves very well to a simple design which can be embroidered on a sachet, or painted on a container.

Other herbs which are the most suitable for herb pillows and cushions are:

Thyme	Southernwood
Lemon Verbena	Marjoram
Sage	Woodruff
Lavender	Angelica
Rose petals	Bergamot
Mint	Rosemary

Valerian is another sleep inducing herb which can be introduced in small quantities, but it does have a bitter smell not acceptable to some and should be used very sparingly.

Marjoram is the surprise herb – so often thought of in its culinary connotation. In fact it has great soothing and sedative properties, and a particularly pervasive but subtle aroma which greatly adds to the charm of a herb pillow, as it does to pot-pourri. Oregano, which is a wild marjoram, is more aromatic and has the same sedative properties (it is, however, far more pungent and hot when used for cooking). Here are some suggested fillings for little sleep pillows, which should be approximately 10″ × 8″ to slip under a pillow or inside the pillow case of the top pillow. Some people prefer to tuck them under their cheek or on top of the pillow.

1. 1 oz. lemon verbena, 1 oz. marjoram, a pinch each of thyme and mint. This is a delightfully non-sweet, clean smelling mixture; a sleep mixture much appreciated by men who do not find it too 'flowery'.

2. 1 oz. lavender, ½ oz. verbena, ½ oz. lemon thyme,

½ oz. woodruff. An old-fashioned cottage smell, good for headaches. Add rosemary (but not for use under the cheek – it can be spiky) and you have a blend which promises peaceful sleep – rosemary was considered by countrywomen to be a specific against nightmares and a little bag of it would be hung on the corner of children's cots to keep away bad dreams.

3. ½ oz. roses and/or peony petals, ½ oz. lavender, ½ oz. mignonette, jonquil or other sweet scented flowers. The peel of an orange dried and ground to powder with 1 desertspoon orris powder.

Make up with lemon verbena to the quantity required to fill a small pillow or scatter cushion. This is a fragrant floral pillow – and the mixture can be enhanced by the addition of rose geranium oil, taking care that it is all well absorbed by the leaves to avoid soiling the cover.

Experiment with these to find your own ideal mixture. A good idea for a present for a sleepless friend is a selection of ingredients, clearly marked, with an attractive sachet or container; he or she can then make up a personally designed sleep-inducing mixture. This would make a delightful present for anyone recovering from illness and confined to bed; for someone really ill, a ready-made sachet is obviously the answer, with the aromas carefully blended to suit the patient and the complaint. An excellent gift for the elderly person, and possibly very welcome also to the mother of a sleepless young baby!

Many people like a spicy smell to their pillow and the addition of powdered clove and/or cinnamon makes an invigorating and interesting filling. Use these powders with great care, however, and sparingly, making sure they are thoroughly mixed in with the leaves, as they tend to

POT
POURRI
herbs
and
spices

POT
POURRI
flowers
for
colour
and
aroma

escape and leave a most unattractive brown dust in their wake. They are also oily powders and can stain fine materials. Their properties are most beneficial in sleep pillows, as they are astringent and head clearing – and have been claimed even to prevent snoring.

Lavender remains the great favourite as a filling for sachets and pillows and is one of the oldest aromatics to be used in this way. It is a powerful antiseptic and is greatly disliked by moths. Moreover, to quote Culpeper 'it is of a special good use for all the griefs and pains of the head and brain that proceed of a cold cause, as the apoplexy, falling-sickness, the dropsy, or sluggish malady, cramps, convulsions, palsies and often faintings. . . . Two spoonfuls of the distilled water of the flowers taken helps them that have lost their voice, as also the tremblings and passions of the heart, and faintings and swoonings, not only being drank, but applied to the temples, or nostrils to be smelled unto and is of so fierce and piercing a quality, that it is cautiously to be used, some few drops being sufficient, to be given with other things, either for inward or outward griefs.'

What better recommendation for its use in sachets and pillows? A sachet filling is also improved by the addition of woodruff, with its nostalgic hay-field smell and its anti-moth propensity, and/or thyme, or southernwood.

A lavender pillow would therefore seem to be a perfect gift for a 'flu victim, and one could go further and make a little cap of lavender as suggested by William Turner in his *New Herball* (1551) – 'I judge that the flower of lavender quilted in a cap and worne are good for all diseases of the head that come from a cold cause and that they comfort the braine very well.'

Here is a more complex and spicy lavender blend – highly aromatic and refreshing. This gives enough for several small sachets:

Hessian dolly bag, embroidered sachets, herb cushions.

2 oz. lavender
1 oz. each thyme, mint and marjoram
1 oz. rose petals
½ oz. orris root powder
½ oz. ground cloves

The clove powder can be replaced by a mixture of ground cinnamon and bruised coriander seeds if preferred.

Lemon verbena is becoming a close runner-up to lavender in popularity – its clean fresh aroma appeals to men who may at first be a little averse to finding sachets among their socks and shirts, but soon become converted. It can be used by itself – it is a crackly large leaved herb and a little goes a long way. You will find it necessary to remove the twigs before filling your pillow or sachet.

Sweet bags

'Sweet Bag' is the old name for a small sachet, usually in the shape of a little bag gathered at the top and having a loop of ribbon. These were used for coat hangers, or to hang in wardrobes, on the backs of doors, at the back of armchairs, and under the 'antimacassa'. They might be filled with a lavender mixture as already given, or with a mixture of geranium leaves of different scents dried and pounded with orris root powder, or with one of the following spicy herb mixtures. The quantities allow for several sachets:

SWEET SACHET

2 oz. rosemary flowers
2 oz. orris root powder
½ oz. powdered nutmeg
The dried petals of a few clove pinks, wallflowers or jonquils

ROSE SACHET

8 oz. whole rose petals
2 oz. geranium leaves or lemon verbena leaves
10 drops rose oil
2 oz. sandalwood raspings

SPICED ROSE SACHET

2 oz. each rose petals and lavender flowers
1 oz. orris root powder
2 teaspoons each of cloves, allspice and cinnamon

LEMON VERBENA SACHET

2 oz. dried and pounded orange and lemon peel
4 oz. lemon verbena
10 drops lemon verbena oil
10 drops oil of bergamot

For the kitchen

A larger version of these sweet bags can be made for the kitchen, containing a specially suitable mixture. The following one contains mint, which deters flies, – as does a bunch of fresh mint hung from the light or in a vase.

KITCHEN SACK

3 oz. lemon verbena
2 oz. dried mint, of mixed scents if possible
(or 1 oz. peppermint or spearmint)
1 oz. lovage
A few cloves and a small piece of orris root

Hessian, which is available in the most attractive vegetable dye colours, makes an ideal material for these sacks. A toning or contrasting cord run through a wide hem at the top will enable the sack to be hung at some convenient spot in the kitchen, preferably where one will be tempted to squeeze it occasionally on passing by. As with all sachets, the aroma is released with renewed strength when handled or moved about.

Some other herbs which are deterrent to flies and can well be incorporated in mixtures of 'green herbs' for kitchen sacks or aromatic sweet bags for kitchen clothes lines or dressers are:

Peppermint	Mugwort	Pennyroyal
Basil	Anise	Tansy
Chamomile		Costmary

'Air freshener' herbs to accompany these are bay, rosemary and thyme.

Tansy was one of the favourite medieval strewing herbs because of its power of repelling both flies and fleas, and so efficacious was it that the flowers were rubbed all over joints of meat to keep away the blow-flies, incidentally imparting a flavour which was greatly liked and was said to resemble a mixture of nutmeg and cinnamon. Its spicy scent makes it a good addition to pot-pourri, and it has numerous medicinal virtues.

There are other sweet-smelling presents for the kitchen, using various combinations of these herbs which, being savoury rather than sweet, blend happily with cooking smells.

KITCHEN DRAWER SACHET

This should be about 6″ × 4″, or a square, according to the pattern of the material, which might be one of the many pretty cotton prints intended for kitchen curtains and depicting fruit, flowers or herbs or tiles. These are good to put in dresser drawers, scenting the tea-towels and dusters, and one makes a pleasing little extra to give with a pretty tea-towel.

OVEN-GLOVES

These could match the drawer sachet, and are improved by the inclusion of some of the 'green herbs' mixture or lemon verbena with the wadding. Lemon verbena is particularly effective in combating greasy smells, and a bowl of it, with some mint and a bay leaf and a few dried nasturtiums for colour goes well on the windowsill.

Sachets

For people who are averse to sewing there is a form of sachet which can contain any of the foregoing blends – though it is important to ensure that all oilness is fully absorbed by the herbs and orris root. These are simply paper envelopes, preferably of the fairly thick coloured kind, resembling hand-made paper. These can be decorated with a drawing of a spray of herbs, or a pressed sprig. These envelopes can be placed among stored linen blankets, curtains, etc. One can write on them to the effect that they are 'A spicy sachet for the scenting of linen presses, closets and chests'.

Making pillows and sachets

One of the most satisfying things about making up pillows and sachets of herbs is choosing just the right materials for the cases. Firstly they must be suitable in composition, being materials that can 'breathe'. This not only allows the aroma of the herbs to escape to be appreciated but keeps the herbs in the right condition. Therefore pure cotton or silk are ideal; man-made fabrics are not suitable. It is quite hard to smell herbs through the latter and in time they seem to have an unsatisfactory effect on the herbs, changing their character in a way which is quite different from the natural fading of the original smell. An old sachet found in an attic, packed in grandmother's wedding dress, will not smell as it did when first it was made but will have an indefinable fragrant, subtle mustiness which is entirely pleasing whereas a sachet made of nylon or rayon if left in a drawer for some time will have undergone a surprising synthesis which quite takes away its original charm.

I would make one exception to this; quite the most charming and old world material for small lavender bags is muslin or organdie – the latter being particularly suitable for embroidery. It is hard to find cotton organdie today and I have found the modern equivalent satisfactory. Another exception is net, which makes very pretty sachets used doubly and edged with lace. Today it is nearly always made of nylon but its porous nature allows the pot-pourri filling to breathe. Some of the colourful pot-pourris are particularly pretty enclosed in dress net; it is interesting to find that some shades enhance flower colours much more than others. Try coffee brown, purple, dark green and flame. Pale blue, pale green and pink dim the flower colours most strangely. Where the net is coarse, two layers may need to be used, for it is important to ensure that fragments do not escape; if there is a tendency to this with any material you use, try a lining of fine net or muslin.

Another consideration in choosing cottons, linens and silks is the suitability of the design, and there is endless fun to be had in tracking down the right patterns for your pillows and sachets. Cotton includes not only dress materials but calico, denim, ginghams (these three lend themselves very well to embroidery), furnishing fabrics, lawns or voile – plain or embroidered, and lace. Any material that is washable has an advantage – the contents are of course emptied before washing and replaced. Silk and linen are both expensive to buy new but there are often remnants to be had at some of the big stores. A more economical source of both linen and silk, in many cases of a far better quality than one sees today, are sale rooms and attics. Old linen sheets and pillow slips have a luxurious feel, as do old dresses, camisoles and nighties made up of fine batiste cotton or of silk. An antique silk wedding dresses might make twenty or more priceless and unique sachets.

Bundles of old lace can sometimes be purchased on oddment stalls at markets and make exquisite small sachets and sweet bags; if the design is large they will need to be lined. Very often a piece of lace or a length of silk will suggest the pillow to you.

Herb pillows to give to young people look fresh and countrified in tiny cotton prints. A favourite aunt might prefer a rose covered chintz in colours to match her bedroom. Calico has a crisp country look to it; pinked at the edges and sewn with a coloured chain or stem stitch, perhaps embroidered with a name or a small herb design, it can look as though it were lovingly made in a Victorian vicarage.

Sachet cases can be made either by hand or with the sewing machine. You need not always keep to the traditional square or oblong shape; try a hexagon or circle; a Christmas star or a heart for St Valentine's Day; more adventurously, an initial, if this is suitable, or, if you are using a large-patterned chintz or cotton, follow the outline of a flower motif.

Where you can, attach a little loop of ribbon or cord to the sachet, in case it is to be hung up. Decorate your sachets as you wish; handkerchief lace makes a pretty edging for muslin or organdie, many forms of embroidery and appliqué can be used; patchwork can be very pretty, if the colours of pieces are well chosen and if they are not too large.

More ideas

Once one starts filling little pillows with herbs one's ideas expand. Why not fill a simple muslin bag with the herbs of one's choice, with lemon verbena or lavender and insert it inside a favourite cushion cover? Why not make a shaped cushion about 15″ long by 8″ deep using kapok or an acrylic wadding, and insert a muslin bag at each end to make a restful aromatic neck pillow to support and comfort the neck when reading or watching the television?

An old Victorian idea was to attach a small herb pillow to a long straight piece of the same material which hung over the back of an armchair, with a small lead weight at each end to keep it in position. Similarly, sweet bags were hung from the arms of chairs. Don't stop at chair cushions, those popular enormous floor cushions can likewise be treated to a large flat muslin-covered lemon verbena pad inside the cover – on the upper side. The gentle waft of lemon verbena will surprise the descending sitter.

Herb blends as fillings have many other domestic uses, but one which is a development of the sweet bag hung from a coathanger is the herb coathanger. These can be made a little more special by inserting lavender or lemon verbena or one of the sweet bag mixtures already mentioned inside the cover. Strips of wadding make good padding and the herbs can be interspersed in the strips before the cover is put on; a small looped sachet of matching herbs can be attached to the hook. Choose a pretty flower or herb sprig material with a fairly small pattern and it is easy and convenient to make up complementary accessories with a matching fragrance. Shoe bags in the roomy dolly-bag shape can have the herbs inserted inside the circular base; this has the added benefit of making it firmer. Envelope shaped bags of various sizes with a herb filled back would take tights, nighties and so on for packing. A night dress case accompanied by a sleep pillow filled with the same blend will give both night dress and the room an illusive delicate scent. The possibilities are endless – night dress case, hot water bottle cover and handkerchief sachet, or a brush and comb bag, all these sets are made rather special by the addition of fragrant herbs.

4

Herb teas

One of the nicest ways to give herbs as presents is in collections. Freshly dried and therefore of good colour and aroma, they can be packed in cellophane bags, sealed and boxed in sets, either in gift boxes bought for the purpose or in pretty chocolate or sweet boxes which you have kept, or in open baskets such as can be purchased cheaply from shops specialising in imported craft goods, or the basketware departments of most stores; the latter containers become useful afterwards as bread baskets.

Herb teas can be packed in this way, and it is helpful to write inside the lid of the box, or on a card, simple instructions for making herb tea – and indeed it is a very simple procedure.

A tisane from dried leaves or flowers

1. Warm a china, pottery or glass jug or teapot – (don't use metal).
2. Place 1 heaped teaspoon for each cup into the vessel.
3. Pour boiling water over the herb or flowers.
4. Allow to infuse for 8 minutes only.
5. Strain into cup. Sweeten with a little clear honey (acacia is recommended) if desired.

Herb tea collection: a good introductory selection

ROSE HIP TEA: rich in Vitamin C and with a fruity flavour.

PEPPERMINT TEA: soothing, digestive, a delightful evening drink.

SAGE TEA: stimulating, and excellent against coughs and sore throats.

CHAMOMILE TEA: a delicately aromatic and digestive tea.

NETTLE TEA: one of the oldest of English countryside teas and rich in iron; may be sweetened with honey, lemon may be added. It can be deliciously combined with China tea and served with lemon.

Herb tea collection for poor sleepers

1. CHAMOMILE: a soothing digestive drink after dinner.
2. LIMEFLOWERS: tranquillising, with a delicious flavour.
3. VALERIAN: a sleep inducing tea from a dried root, rather bitter but improved by honey.
4. LEMON VERBENA TEA: a fragrant and sedative tea – can be taken with mint tea.
5. HOPS: a nerve soothing tea with a pleasant taste – a specific for insomnia.
6. BERGAMOT TEA: a sleep inducing tea, which can be added to China or Indian tea.

Herb Teas for Beauty

1. ROSEMARY: for clear eyes and sight.
2. HORSETAIL: for strong nails and hair.
3. YARROW: for cleansing the system.
4. ROSEMARY: stimulates the growth and improves the condition of hair.
5. SAGE: a valuable tonic which improves the circulation – combines well with mint to make a refreshing and restorative drink.

6. LEMON BALM TEA: a fine early morning tea to cheer and uplift, to counteract stress and brighten the eyes.

Many of these herbs may be found growing wild, or in your own garden, and can be dried as previously described, but all can be purchased from herbalists and specialist suppliers. Buy them loose by the ounce whenever possible, so that you can see that the colour is bright; if you ask to smell them before they are packaged you can ensure the aroma is strong and fresh. In fairness, however, remember that there is a season for herbs as for all growing things, and if you are buying in the early months of the year you must expect last year's crop; if shelved, as is usual, in large airtight storage jars there should be no serious deterioration.

Blends

There are some delightful teas made from blends of two or more herbs, and these make delightful small presents if attractively packed. Some suggestions (from a stillroom book of 1839) are: 'Dried Hawthorn Leaves 2 parts, Sage and Lemon Balm mixed 1 part' – a delicate tea to bring peace and calm.

Here are some more:

A TEA FOR SLEEP: limeflowers, chamomile, 2 parts of each to 1 part bergamot (not essential).

TO RELIEVE A HEADACHE: rosemary with lavender flowers in equal parts.

A TONIC TEA: peppermint and yarrow in equal parts.

A TEA WITH A 'CHINA' FLAVOUR: strawberry or raspberry leaves, to which add an equal quantity of thyme or lemon thyme.

A SUBTLE 'COMBINATION' TEA: to a good brand of green tea ('Gunpowder tea' is particularly suitable) add per half

'There are some delightful teas made from blends of two or more herbs . . .'

pound (a) an ounce each of mint and lemon thyme, or (b) 2 oz. each of elderflower and rose petals, or (c) jasmine or orange blossom with limeflowers.

A tea recommended to help the person who is trying to stop smoking may or may not be a popular present. It is a blend of lady-slipper, scullcap, valerian, catnip and peppermint, all available from herbalists and said to be a very safe and calming sedative, which has a strengthening action on the central nervous system.

Perhaps also you could risk giving a good herbal smoking mixture! It consists of equal parts of coltsfoot and chamomile with the same quantity together of lemon thyme, rosemary and eyebright. If smoked in a pipe, a very little honey may be added. The wonderful herb comfrey, known for its great healing properties, can also be smoked enjoyably in a pipe and has a soothing effect on the lungs. Which leads to:

A TEA FOR THE SMOKER: This will help to relieve smoker's throat. Equal parts of hyssop, horehound, coltsfoot and marshmallow root. Make a strong tea of 2 teaspoons per cup, and add honey to sweeten.

5

Culinary collections and blends

Spice racks are probably the most familiar way of giving herb collections for the kitchen, but they are expensive, the herbs contained in them are not always of the freshest available and the different flavours are usually confined to the basics. An adventurous cook would appreciate a less conservative assortment, and according to the resources of your garden, your wild herb discoveries, or your discerning purchases, here are some useful and more unusual collections which can be packeted in cellophane and attractively boxed as with the teas. You can of course use many other kinds of packaging, charming old kitchen utensils which you have found or modern, practical wares which are enhanced by their contents – a colander or saucepan, perhaps.

Make your choice of three or four or more from the selection according to what is available.

Soup herbs

CHICKEN: balm, chervil, lavender, tarragon, thyme, sorrel.
BEEF OR OXTAIL: basil, chervil, marjoram, sorrel, lovage, coriander seeds, sweet cicely.

MUSHROOM: fennel, basil, tarragon, oregano.
POTATO, LEEK AND POTATO, WATERCRESS: marjoram, dill, anise, nasturtium, lemon or apple mint.
TOMATO: basil, lavender, chives, thyme, oregano.
PEA OR LENTIL: costmary, sorrel, savory, chervil.
ONION: sage, thyme, oregano.

Vinegar Herbs

These can be made up and bottled attractively or given as a collection of vinegar herbs for the discerning cook. They are to be used with the best quality white vinegar. About 2 oz. herbs or flowers should be added to 1 pint of vinegar, tightly corked and left for about 3 weeks – preferably in sunlight – strained and bottled.

HERBS SUITABLE FOR VINEGARS
Tarragon; elderflower; chives; mint; winter savory with balm; basil; thyme and lemon thyme; sage; oregano.

Vinegar spices

These should be simmered for 5 minutes in 1 pint white vinegar and then strained and bottled. 1 teaspoon each of white sugar, black peppercorns, celery seeds, cloves. ½ teaspoon ground ginger, 2 chillies.

Sauce Herbs

Dill and fennel (for fish).
Tarragon and Parsley (for fowl).
Bergamot (for pork).

Salad Herbs

Chives, thyme, tarragon and sorrel (for egg dishes).
Chervil, lavender, mint, coriander seed, caraway and dill (for green salads).
Savory, caraway, sweet cicely, sorrel (for potato salads).
Basil, oregano, chives and savory (for tomato salads).

Broth Herbs

A jar of blended herbs for adding to English casseroles and stews is made from equal parts of parsley, thyme and rosemary.

Spices

Packs of peppercorns and coarse salt, boxed with pepper and salt mills, make very good, if unsurprising, presents. There are however, some nice variations which can be given with or without a mill. Mix and wrap equal quantities of: black peppercorns, white peppercorns, allspice berries and coriander seeds. Black and white peppers only make 'Mignonette Pepper'. A delicious seasoning can be made and packed in a jar or given with a pepper pot. This mixture is as follows: Grind two ounces each of black and white pepper together, add a little ground cinnamon, allspice and paprika. Experiments will lead you to other tasty blends. Black peppers always seem particularly acceptable and no enthusiastic users ever have enough. One rather intriguing way to pack these for a gift is to make a 'dolly bag' of some colourful stiff material. The gathering tape or braid should have a long loop for hanging in the larder or kitchen.

A gourmet spice collection

black peppers
mace blades
juniper berries
poppy seeds
paprika

fennel seeds
a nutmeg
a vanilla pod
a stick of cinnamon

2 oz. or 4 oz. cellophane packets of the spices and berries are suitable, with the pod, the stick and the nutmeg wrapped separately and laid between them. The mixture

of spice colours is most pleasing to the eye and encouraging to the cook. A good accompaniment to this box is a copy of a good book on cookery with spices, such as Elizabeth David's *Spices, Salt and Aromatics in the English Kitchen.*

Your favourite curry recipe book, of which there are many in paperback editions could accompany the following:

A curry collection

coriander seeds
turmeric
cumin seed
fenugreek
mustard seed
black pepper
dried chillies
poppy seed
cardamons
cinnamon
ginger, powdered

Most people have their favourite curry recipes or like to experiment, and this collection gives them the opportunity. But there is one powder which it is simple to make up in your mortar; it is delightfully aromatic and appetising and can be given to a friend whom you know to 'collect curries'. I am indebted to Rosemary Hemphill for this excellent powder, taken from her book *Herbs and Spices.*

1 dessertspoon ground cinnamon
1 teaspoon ground cloves
1 dessertspoon ground ginger
1 dessertspoon fenugreek seed
1 dessertspoon mustard seed
1 tablespoon chilli powder
1 tablespoon ground coriander

1 tablespoon turmeric
1 dessertspoon cumin seed
2 teaspoons cardamon seed

Grind and blend all ingredients together. Keep in an air-tight jar. The addition of a few whole cloves is suggested which adds to the irresistible aroma.

Elizabeth David mentions two interesting points in connection with curry which I think are worth passing on.

1. When using curry powder, particularly a ready made one, the flavour will be greatly improved if the powder is heated on a heatproof plate in a low oven for a few minutes before using, and

2. Do not forget the salt. The latter seems absurdly obvious and yet I realise how many curry recipes fail to mention it and how essential it is to bring out the flavours of the spices.

Seasoned salt

Another appetising blend may be ground together in your mortar, to make a herb and spice salt:

1 teaspoon celery salt
1 teaspoon rosemary
a pinch of mace
a pinch of paprika
1 tablespoon salt

Other herbs and spices may be crushed and added to salt to make a variety of appetising seasonings.

Flowers for cooking

A most decorative and appealing collection is made from flowers for the cook. Best and most useful of them is

Some yellow colouring agents – saffron, tumeric and marigold

the marigold. Whole heads may be added to stews and casseroles, the petals scattered on salads, or cooked with rice to give a rich yellow tinge.

SAFFRON

Marigolds have already been mentioned as a flavouring agent for rice. The classic ingredient for this is of course saffron, that rare and costly product from the yellow crocus. This is indeed a precious and appreciated gift. Beware of buying the 'powdered' saffron – it is of inferior quality and may even be diluted. Find the little reddish yellow threads, which are the stamens of the crocus. Probably you will buy them in little cellophane envelopes. About ¼ oz. is a generous present as you need only three or four threads to a pint of rice. Two lovely ways to pack this precious commodity is (a) in a pretty thimble, either an old one you can buy or a modern plastic one which you can paint with small flowers or herbs. (b) in half a walnut shell, secured with 'cling-wrap'.

For those who think this too extravagant, somewhere between saffron and marigold in price is turmeric. Two teaspoons of turmeric are enough to give the classic yellow colour to rice and so a little jar of 4 oz. would be a useful quantity to give.

Flower collections for cooks

Elderflowers for fritters
Marigolds for stews
Dandelions for salads
Rose petals for butter and for vinegar
Violets for crystallising and for salads
Nasturtiums for salads and for vinegar

Another idea for crystallising at home: If you have angelica growing in your garden or can find it growing wild it is very simple to candy, and worth doing as it is most expensive to buy. Cut the young stalks into 10 cm. lengths, lie them singly in a pan (none should overlap) and cover with boiling sugar syrup, leave for 24 hours then drain the stems, reboil the syrup and pour again on to the stems. Leave again for 24 hours. Repeat once more leaving the stems in the syrup until they are bright, light green and well glazed.

Bouquet Garni

Individual bouquets garni can be bought today in little muslin bags with a tape attached – a useful and convenient additive to stews and casseroles, and one which you can easily make yourself to give, packaging half a dozen or so together. However, far more ornamental are sprigs of classic bouquet garni, without the muslin, tied securely with fine strong thread and boxed; these are particularly pleasant if made from freshly dried herbs from your garden:

1 bay leaf
2 sprigs parsley with stalks
1 sprig thyme.

Seasonable Gifts

One that suggests Christmas fare is an onion and a lemon, both well stuck with cloves. They can be put together (each wrapped in foil), in a little net stocking. The onion is for the bread sauce and the lemon for the mulled ale! Another spice mixture which can be readily mixed in your stillroom and which makes a helpful present for the house or cook is:

MULLED ALE SPICES

1 dessertspoon each of good nutmeg, ground cloves and ground ginger. This mixture is recommended by Mrs Beeton in her *Book of Household Management*, to be

used one teaspoon at a time to each quart of good ale, to which should be added a glass of rum or brandy and a tablespoon of sugar.

Herb Sugars

These flavoured sugars need to be prepared from five to six weeks before they are to be given as gifts and they are particularly acceptable to the busy cook who will be delighted to have ready to hand flavoured sugars for her milk puddings, junkets, cakes and so on. Into a pound of castor sugar in a pretty jar (which can be decorated), put a vanilla pod broken into two, well in the centre of the sugar where it will do its work through the weeks imparting a delicate aromatic flavouring. The same can be done with leaves of rose geranium, lemon mint spearmint; the jars should of course be prettily labelled and dated so that the cook knows when they have 'matured'.

Herb Butter

This is easily prepared, and can be pressed into small honey jars or paté pots and covered with a ring of greaseproof paper and a gingham or flowered cotton cap, pinked round the edges and fastened with ribbon over an elastic band.

Cream 4 oz. of unsalted butter, add ½ teaspoon lemon juice then blend in 1 oz. finely chopped herbs – parsley, mint, lovage, tarragon or a combination of any of these.

Herb Jellies

These are an expensive delicatessen purchase, but a cheat's way to make them secretly in your stillroom is to use commercial packets of dessert jelly, made up according to the instructions on the box; before they set, add your herbs. To 1 pint of orange add 2 tablespoons finely chopped rose geranium leaves and/or lemon thyme. To a lemon jelly add marjoram or mint, to a lime jelly add savory. Then experiment with other flavours and the herbs you have available. If you prefer to make your own jelly, use fresh fruit and gelatine; or apple jelly makes a very good basis for most herbs.

Jellies for parties

These can be made to look really special if you arrange sprigs and sprays of herbs and flowers in a pattern. You will need to make up the jellies with less water than usual so that they are very stiff. Pour a little into the mould first and allow to set really firmly. Then make your design, and pour in the rest of the jelly when it is cool and at setting point. Good herbs and flowers to use for this are borage, violet, comfrey, Roman chamomile, anchusa, marigolds, nasturtium, angelica flower, mint. You can use your artistry to blend suitable colours with the jelly used.

Herb ice cubes

Fill your freezer tray with water to which the juice of a lemon has been added and put a spring of mint into each division. The cubes look most cooling and pretty in a long drink.

Herb Stuffing

This colourful blend is suitable for a pretty jar and should be labelled 'Special Herb Stuffing'. Blend in ½ oz. of soft butter before using.

1 tsp. chopped chive
1 tsp. dried sage
½ tsp. dried thyme
½ tsp. dried marjoram
a pinch of salt
a pinch of pepper
4 heaped tablespoons of white bread crumbs
the grated peel of one lemon
¼ tsp. of turmeric (optional)

A Cook's Cracker

This is just for fun but most cooks are very glad to receive a cracker from the Christmas Tree which has been made up with pretty paper around a vanilla pod, a stick of angelica and a cinnamon stick, each one wrapped separately in cellophane. The idea can of course be adapted using other suitable herbs or spices.

6

Herb cards, bookmarks and other flights of fancy

The collection of herbs and spices in your stillroom will become so interesting and appealing to the eye that you will want to do more with them than mix them into things to be drunk, eaten or smelt. The shapes and colours of herbs are fascinating in design, and seem to lend themselves to pressing and arranging as much as the more usual flowers. The various jars, packages and boxes so far described are enhanced if they are accompanied by a card giving a list of the contents, simple recipes or other relevant information. If you have kept some particularly fine sprigs of thyme or flowers of chamomile, marjoram, or other herbs, these can be pressed and arranged in groups on your cards. Attach them by using a fine pair of tweezers. Use an adhesive such as 'Cow Gum', a transparent rubber solution. This allows you to move the plants a little when arranging them in natural curving positions. Use the gum very sparingly, applying it to the surface of the plant to be stuck with an orange stick or match stick. When the arrangement meets with your satisfaction, press down on to the card over the arrangement with a clean piece of blotting paper.

Smaller sprigs can be used in the same way to decorate

Pomander, tussy-mussy posy, book marks and cards

gift tags and also bookmarks, which can convey a useful herb recipe or hint. It is possible to buy sheets of transparent sealing material, and you may like to use these to protect your design, covering the whole card or bookmark.

If you prefer, and if you have mastered the technique, you could draw the herbs, using pen and ink or watercolour; or you could make a lino block and print off your cards. More simply made is a potato cut, and the simplicity and yet the characteristic shapes of herb leaves make them particularly suitable for reproducing in this way, which most of us learnt at school.

The two latter methods have the advantage that as well as being used to stamp out gift tags they can be printed on to calico which you can use to make small sacks or dolly bags to hold gifts of herbs, spices etc.

It is also amusing to find herbs with meanings to convey messages on your cards. These can be either pressed or drawn and I give below a list reversed from the usual in that it shows the meaning first, before the name of the various flowers or herbs that have been used in past times to convey a message.

Love	Basil, cedarwood, myrtle, pansies, red rose, single pink, tulip
Devotion	Heliotrope, honeysuckle
Fidelity	Cumin, forget-me-not, ivy, veronica
Infidelity	Daisy, larkspur, yellow rose
Compassion, consolation	Balm, elderflower, poppy
Gratitude	Campanula
Joy	Burnet, jasmine, marigold, marjoram, parsley, saffron
Sorrow	Hyacinth, primrose, yew
Glory	Bay leaf, laurel

Silence	Belladonna, lavender, white rose
Remembrance	Everlasting flower, heartsease, marigold, rosemary, syringa
Unexpected meeting	Lemon geranium
Expected meeting	Pimpernel
Hope	Almond blossom, hawthorn
Thought	Pansy
Modesty	Violet
Escape	Pennyroyal
Courage	Borage
Purity	Clematis, lily, lily-of-the-valley, sweet briar
Humility, patience	Chamomile, rosebud
Happiness	Jasmine

Another way of sending a living message is to make a posy of the herbs and flowers – these are at least as pretty as a conventional bouquet and can be given with a pot or jar to hold them. This is particularly acceptable to friends in hospital as it can stand by their bed side, and there is not the usual problem of finding a vase for them.

A posy of past times which is fun to make today is known as a 'Tussie Mussie'. These were carried in times past to ward off evil spirits and as an antiseptic against the plague and other ills. In the early days Tussie Mussies always included the herbs with the highest claims to combating germs and smells – rosemary, thyme, southernwood and lavender. To this day they are carried in front of the judge when he enters the court, in memory of times when he had to contend with noxious smells and diseases. In Victorian times they became pretty posies for special occasions or to carry sentimental messages. They are very much a part of English tradition and many old cottage gardens still have a Tussie Mussie bed of suitable small flowers. Queen Elizabeth II was handed a Tussie Mussie as she entered Westminster Abbey for her Coronation, and there seems no reason why this pretty custom should not continue to give pleasure.

Start your Tussie Mussie in the centre with a small but perfect bud such as a rose bud. Then build circles around it of tiny flowers alternating with herbs. Suitable flowers such as forget-me-nots, batchelor's buttons, chamomile, sage, rosemary, mignonette, primrose, heartsease, violets, clove pinks and lavender can be used, or make a completely herbal Tussie Mussie.

Another traditional gift which has been made in cottage homes for centuries and for the same functional reason, in that it was carried to ward off germs and to mask unpleasant smells, is the orange pomander. This is made from a small orange pierced all over with cloves. Many people like to make these today but I feel a warning should be given that they are not as easy as they look. The orange you choose should be of the size that you wish the finished and dried pomander to be (about 6″ circumference is usual). The cloves must be of the very best quality you can obtain; the excellent big headed Zanzibar cloves we used to use are unfortunately almost impossible to find, but choose the strongest and largest you can obtain and be certain that the heads are undamaged and the stems are not broken.

1. Roll the orange around in your hand – it will be easier to stick the cloves into the warm and softened skin.

2. Stick the cloves into your orange very evenly leaving the space of a head between each head of clove; this will close up as the orange shrinks, and if this space is not left it will prevent the proper drying of the centre of the orange. If the orange has a tough skin, it may be a good

idea to make preliminary holes for the cloves with the point of a fine knitting needle.

3. Roll the cloved orange in a mixture of powdered orris root, cinnamon and clove and place in an airing cupboard or similar warm and airy place. Dry very slowly indeed. If they are put in too warm a cupboard or in a humid heat they will get mildew. If they are dried too fast the outside will become very hard and brittle but the inside will eventually go rotten.

4. Then the pomander can if desired be painted or sprayed with an aromatic oil (such as musk or clove carnation) but must then be given more drying time before being circled with a narrow ribbon, allowing a 6″ loop at the top.

Unfortunately due to the quality of cloves today it is sometimes impossible to complete the pomander without loosing some of the heads and spoiling the look. A good way out of this difficulty is to cut a square of coloured net or a combination of two squares in say coffee and orange or red and green. Place the pomander in the centre of the square, draw the net up around it and tie with a narrow ribbon leaving a 6″ loop. The four points of the square will stick up stiffly and look very pretty when the pomander is hanging.

7

Herbal properties and presents

Herbs and flowers have been used in our stillroom so far for their sweet smells and their culinary uses but they have all sorts of other characteristics and potentials. Every herb that you find and study has various properties and qualities and quite often when you think you have read all about it from one source you will find yet more intriguing items of folk lore or history from another book or early pamphlet. There are some well proven attributes of certain herbs that particularly fit them for gifts of a different sort.

SWEET CICELY

for instance, one of the *umbelliferae* family, lives up to its name and does indeed sweeten any dish to which it is added. Unfortunately it is hard to find wild but grows in many gardens and can be bought, cut and dried. A jar of it makes a good present for a diabetic or for somebody you know to be watching their diet. It should be used weight for weight with sugar to halve the quantity of sugar needed. As an added benefit it has the reputation among country people that it cures gastric upsets.

BASIL

That most deliciously aromatic of herbs, loved by cooks, has also the property of clearing the head and a stuffy nose and for this reason was at one time added to snuff, so it is a good additive to sleep pillows. It is also used to relieve headaches so that very acceptable little sachets or sweet bags of it can be made to give to sufferers with sinus trouble to carry in their handbags and to sniff when the need arises. Not proven but on ancient record is the belief that it is also an aphrodisiac!

In Italy a sprig of basil is an emblem of love and fidelity and in some parts of Europe it is worn to ward off the evils of witchcraft. It has a smell which appeals very strongly to some people and it blends quite happily with lemon verbena or lavender. For any of the foregoing reasons it can be included in some of the little toys mentioned later in this chapter.

Herbs have been used during the centuries to fight infection, noxious smells, fleas, lice and similar pests and it has already been suggested that wormwood, woodruff or southernwood make good additions to sachets for blanket chests, linen rooms, etc., as they are repellent to moths. There are other herbs which deter other pests and can be usefully employed.

RUE

An ancient and much favoured herb, which despite its rather bitter taste and smell has long been known as the Herb of Grace. It was one ingredient of an antiseptic against the Great Plague known as 'Four Thieves Vinegar' – a preparation made of sage, rosemary, rue, wormwood and lavender in vinegar.

Herbs for animals

Rue has also been found very effective against fleas which makes it ideal for putting either inside a dog pillow or in a little sachet to keep in the dog basket. He won't eat it – he won't like the taste. Unfortunately it is no good including it in the cat pillow described later on in this chapter. Cats do not like it at all and will keep away from it.

CATMINT (also called Catnip and Catnep)

A particularly pretty border herb but many gardeners will have noticed sadly that their fine bushes have been squashed down in the middle to form a cosy nest for their cat. I love to see a contented cat lying, sunning itself, surrounded by the lovely mauve spikes and blissfully inhaling the aroma. Gerard in his Herball of 1636 says of cat mint or 'Nep' that 'the later Herbarists doe call it Herba Cattaria, and Herba Catti, because cats are very much delighted herewith; for the smell of it is so pleasant unto them, that they rub themselves upon it, and wallow or tumble in it, and also feed on the branches and leaves very greedily.'

A little pillow to fit a cat's basket is looked upon with much favour by the most pernickety of cats. It really has a powerful effect, so very little is needed, and I suggest that it is mixed with lemon verbena, say 1 tablespoon of the former to 2 oz. of the latter, and enclosed in a muslin bag inside the pillow case. A purpose-made pillow to fit the basket in a pretty washable fabric can contain this mixture enclosed in terylene wadding as a filling. For good measure some dried wormwood can be included. It is hated by fleas and tolerated cheerfully by cats. If cats are already affected dried wormwood can be rubbed into the coat and then brushed out. This will get rid of any fleas,

'There are countless ideas for herbal presents . . .'

usually without annoying the cat in any way, as do some of the proprietary powders on the market.

Mention of catmint brings to mind a present for cats – a catmint mouse. The most rudimentary shape will suffice but the material must be tough and tightly sewn. If it has one tablespoon of catmint in it and a long string tail it will give hours of entertainment and joy to your cat and get rid of all his aggressions. Calico is an excellent material, being tough, and the addition of little felt ears and two bead eyes will please the owner even if the cat doesn't care.

For children

Charming herbal toys for children can also be made; patterns for mice and many other creatures are not difficult to obtain (see the list of suppliers at back of this book for details). Some patterns lend themselves more readily than others to herb fillings. Simple two dimensional designs are best for this purpose, tiny flat kittens, frogs, fish, rabbits and puppies or elephants with floppy ears make sachets that are popular, and not only with children. Lavender is an obvious favourite for filling but lemon verbena with a touch of basil, thyme or mint is more unusual and is greatly enjoyed. Herbs can be tucked into the tummies of the animals, into the ears of the floppy-eared ones and in any place where they will attract an affectionate squeeze – herbs give much more generously of their aroma if they are handled and warmed and squeezed by the hand, particularly in the case of little toys which include stuffing as well. Most patterns can be made to various scales, and of course you can invent your own designs. Thus your kitten can become a cushion-sized cat, its tummy bulging enticingly with lemon verbena. For floppy animals which can be pushed into any position, a filling of tiny polystyrene balls mixed with herbs gives a delightful fragrance.

Children love things that smell. Rag dolls can have lavender in their pockets or mob caps and they appreciate a little pillow or pyjama case of their own filled with a blend of lavender and rosemary. The traditional shaped lavender bag is an easy early sewing exercise for young children and they love to fill them with simple mixtures of lavender and thyme or mint.

Certain types of pot-pourri have a greater lasting quality than others depending on the type of fixatives and oils used and it is possible to make a blend that will not have a particularly colourful appearance but a potent and lasting fragrance. If this is to be used for the next two ideas I suggest mixing highly scented roses, mignonette or carnations, thyme, scented leaved geraniums, crushed bay leaf, a generous amount of grated lemon or grated orange peel (all pith removed) and both powdered orris root and gum benzoin. Two wild herbs, woodruff and ladies-bed-straw make a good addition because these are two herbs which strengthen in scent when they are dried. A few drops of oil of musk or oil of heliotrope may be added and very well blended one drop at a time so that absolutely no oiliness remains discernible. This is a very good mixture to put into china pomanders, and a particular use is the perfuming of other articles.

More ideas

HERB SCENTED LINING PAPER

At least a quart of pot-pourri, preferably more, should be spread in a dress box with a lid. Into this can be laid small rolls of wallpaper or gift paper. This can be left for as long as possible with occasional turning and will gradually absorb the smell so that you have scented drawer paper, and afterwards, a bowl of matching pot-pourri. Cheap wallpaper which often has quite a pretty floral design is preferable to good gift wrapping paper only because it has a more absorbent quality. Other things can go in the box – gloves, handkerchiefs, writing paper.

HERB SCENTED WRITING PAPER seems to be returning to fashion. A box of paper and envelopes can be opened and a small sachet of the above mixture or one of the spicy sweet bag blends can be placed between the envelopes and paper and the box re-wrapped with an attractive ribbon.

SCENTED GARTERS are more of a nonsense present for St Valentine's day than a necessity, but people do wear them and I was surprised how many lavender filled garters were sold following a press mention of them in one of the papers. They are made of wide elastic, not too tight and restricting. This is covered in a tube of pretty lawn or gingham or sprigged voile. Double the circumference of the garter is gathered to fit it; make two lines of stitching, one either side of the elastic, to form a frill. Lavender seems to be the favourite filling but as with all herb gifts the scent can be chosen to suit the recipient.

A HERB CANDLE is a rather less personal gift. There are special candle making kits available (my list of suppliers includes a firm which supplies the necessary materials and also publishes a hand-book on every aspect of candle making). If scented oils are to be added to the wax to enhance the smell of the herbs it is better to buy oils specially intended for this purpose, as the essential oils used in pot-pourri do not always blend correctly with the heated wax. Old candles can be re-used, melted down and poured into any simple containers that may be around the kitchen such as yoghourt pots or cream cartons, using string for the wicks; while the candle is setting, suspend this from a cocktail stick balanced over the top of the pot; the other end of the string should emerge from a small hole in the bottom of the pot. Make sure it is long enough. The old candles should be heated slowly in a strong pan, making certain that the wax does not exceed a temperature of 180° fahrenheit. Tie a fresh bunch of herbs with tape or put dried herbs of your choice in a small muslin bag and leave them in the heated wax over a low heat for about forty minutes. Remove the herbs and pour the wax into the mould, keeping back a small amount. Tear away the mould when the wax is cool and decorate with little sprigs of the herb you have used, fixing them with dabs of warm wax and painting over them with a little warm wax which you have kept back. The proper equipment will give you a more professional effect, and practice will be rewarded with really aromatic and picturesque candles, smelling far more subtle than the synthetically scented ones.

SPICED ROSE BEADS

Mix together in a small jug: 1 oz. glycerin, and ½ oz. oil of rose. Mix together in a bowl 1 oz. powdered gum benzoin, 1 oz. powdered gum acacia, ½ oz. finely chopped vanilla bean, ½ oz. powdered orris root, ½ oz. powdered cinnamon.

Add the contents of the jug to the bowl and stir until a stiff paste is formed. Roll the paste into little balls and allow to dry on the outside sufficiently to handle; pierce a hole in each bead with a hot needle and then put in a warm place to dry completely. Thread them and enjoy their fragrance – they smell all the more when they are worn and become warm.

8

Baths and beauty: herbal scents

It has been said that nature provides an abundance of the herbs which are of the most use to us, and curiously enough it seems that we are often to be seen getting rid of them – or trying to. Nettles, coltsfoot, yarrow, dandelion are just four of the 'weeds' which, quite apart from their medical uses, are of inestimable value to our complexions, and make excellent face washes.

These and other herbs, in either their dried or fresh form, are infused for use, and as they should not be kept long after infusion it is hardly practicable to make these up for gifts. Collections of herbs for beauty-care, however, with instructions, are fun to receive.

The basic recipe for an infusion for lotions and face washes is one ounce of herbs to one pint of water, brought very slowly to near-boiling point in an enamel or earthenware pan with a tight-fitting lid. Do not allow to boil. Remove the pan from the heat, and allow the herbs to brew for at least one hour – overnight is better. These are some of the herbs from which a selection could be made, and which can be used singly or in combination:

LIMEFLOWERS: a complexion tonic, improving the

circulation and acting against wrinkles; slightly bleaching, and antiseptic. Also good for the hair.

NETTLES: full of minerals, a skin corrective. Excellent for the hair.

YARROW: neutralises greasy skins. A hair tonic.

COLTSFOOT: beneficial for a flushed complexion (dilated veins).

MARIGOLD: a cleanser active against acne, scars and rough skin.

ELDERFLOWERS: a great skin-care herb; soothing, healing, slightly bleaching; also good for the eyes.

CHAMOMILE: kind and soothing to ageing skin and for 'weather-soreness'. An excellent rinse for fair hair.

DANDELION: for face packs, and to remove blackheads – use with nettles.

SAGE: an astringent. A good rinse for dark hair; helpful for large pores.

HORSETAIL: antiseptic and tonic. Strengthens nails and hair.

Many of these herbs are also good additions to the bath, and can be used with others in a number of refreshing and beneficial combinations. Dried herbs can be made up into small muslin bags, with an equal quantity of oatmeal, which will give a milky softness to the water when swished about, or when hung from the tap so that the hot water runs through it. Good mixtures for bath bags are:

Chamomile, rosemary and lavender.
Sage, fennel and yarrow.
Peppermint, rosemary and horsetail.
Thyme and lavender.

Lovage added to any of these is a deoderant, and has a delicately pleasing smell of its own.

A mixture of marigold petals, dried lovage, chamomile

flowers and lavender makes a very pretty and sweet-smelling blend to present in a good-looking jar, complete with ready-made muslin bags for the recipient to fill when required. Other sweet-smelling herbs which can be blended in any combinations to your personal taste, and have a mildly tonic effect in the bath, are marjoram, basil, balm, bergamot and rosemary. Small pink rose petals, lavender and thyme make another pretty blend for jars, and are delightfully aromatic. For poor sleepers, the addition of valerian to the favourite mixture will be found mildly sedative and soothing, though it has a slightly bitter aroma.

A foot bath

Lavender steeped in boiling water makes a good foot-bath with instant tonic effect, and sea-salt with an infusion of horsetail is recommended for tired feet.

For the hair

Some of the most satisfying preparations to make in the stillroom are the various combinations of herbs for improving the hair. They are so immediately effective, and so delightful to use. Packets of shampoos and rinses chosen to suit the recipient's hair colour are flattering presents, and look interesting too. The lathering property of the herbal shampoo is provided by that 'country soap' herb – saponaria or soapwort (also known as 'bouncing Bet'). This is combined with chamomile for fair hair, with sage for dark hair, and with rosemary and southernwood for a brightening and conditioning shampoo. A tonic rinse for dark hair is made of sage and rosemary; for fair hair, from chamomile and yarrow. Nettles are a good addition to both these, with limeflowers or fennel.

For your own use, ring the changes with these herbs and you will find a formula which will particularly suit you.

'Some of the most satisfying preparations to make in the stillroom are the various combinations of herbs for improving the hair . . .' – lime flowers, horsetail and fennel.

Toilet Vinegars

These are deliciously old-fashioned and refreshing and are simple to make in the same way that has been used for centuries. Here are two:

LAVENDER VINEGAR

Fill a bottle with lavender flowers to within one inch from the top. Pour in the best wine vinegar to cover the lavender completely. Stand the bottle on a sunny windowsill for two or three weeks, shaking it every day; strain the vinegar off into a jug, refill the bottle with more lavender flowers, cover again with the same vinegar, and leave again. If this infusion is not sufficiently strong, repeat the process once again. This is a most refreshing vinegar for dabbing on the forehead for headaches or travel-sickness.

ROSE VINEGAR

Strongly scented rose petals are covered in white wine, and steeped for a fortnight or until well scented. The bottle should stand in a warm or sunny place, and the vinegar should be strained before use.

Other toilet vinegars can be made in a similar manner from jasmine, violets, lemon verbena, mignonette or scented geranium leaves.

For something a little out-of-the-ordinary, here is a very old recipe for a tooth-paste which has a most unusual and cleansing taste, and leaves the breath fragrant:

8 oz. powdered arrow root
2 oz. powdered orris root
10 drops oil of lemon
5 drops oil of cloves
5 drops oil of bergamot

Essential Oils

These are the concentrated fragrant oils of flowers, herbs, leaves, seeds, barks and roots of aromatic plants, and they have already been mentioned for the part they play in the making of pot-pourri and mixtures for sachets and sweet-bags. A full list of favourites is given in Chapter 1; from these a good basic half-dozen which would delight anyone with a garden, or with an interest in making their own pot-pourri, would be: rose geranium, bergamot, rosemary, lavender, sweet orange *or* lemon verbena, and sandalwood *or* musk (the latter two act also as fixatives).

Oils vary considerably in strength and quality, and therefore in price, so buy from reputable chemists, herbalists or specialist suppliers. They are in any case much more concentrated than any perfume – in fact, some smell quite unpleasantly strong in the bottle. As they contain no alcohol they do not evaporate as perfume does, so testing on one's wrist an oil of something distinctive such as Patchouli may mean you have it with you to the exclusion of all else for the rest of the day. It is best to test essential oils with one of the fingers of testing paper provided by aromatic suppliers, but if these are not available little strips of blotting paper will do, and just one drop of oil on it should give you the true aroma.

In addition to their uses in pot-pourri, these oils have many other attractions. Due to their extreme concentration, they are at their best when diluted in a carrier, such as vegetable oils for massage or a light cologne for perfume, or well-shaken in a little mild shampoo or bubble-bath for the bath. (They can be used neat, but will then leave an oily high-water mark which is hard to clean.) Dilution should be between three and ten drops to the tablespoonful, according to the strength and quality of the oil.

Added to such vegetable oils as almond, avocado, apricot or wheat germ they make wonderfully therapeutic massage oils, and they are also suitable for inhalations and facial steams. They can be placed on cotton wool or muslin for scenting drawers and cupboards; two or three drops of cotton wool rubbed well into the wood of a drawer under the lining paper can be most luxurious; try blending a woody oil and a flower oil for this – say one drop of sandalwood to two of rose, or one of cedarwood to two of mignonette.

An essence is made from an essential oil added to alcohol or wine vinegar, the usual proportion being 1 to 2 oz. of oil to 1 quart of alcohol. An essential oil of strongly aromatic herbs can be made in your stillroom, but it is nearly impossible to achieve the concentration of perfume that you can purchase commercially. The method is to crush the herb very finely in the mortar. Pour $\frac{1}{3}$ of a pint of odourless vegetable oil such as sunflower, together with 1 tablespoon of wine vinegar, on to 2 tablespoons of the powdered herb; this will fill a $\frac{1}{2}$ pint bottle. Place the bottle, tightly corked, in a hot sunny spot for three weeks, and remember to shake it at least daily. At the end of three weeks, strain the herbs off and press all the oil out of them, returning it to the bottle over another freshly crushed 2 tablespoons of herb. This process may have to be repeated again to achieve the strength of perfume you will want. Apart from the unlikelihood of experiencing much continuity of sunshine over a period of three weeks, pressing the oil from the herbs is a messy business. In the absence of enough sunshine, the bottle of oil, vinegar and herbs can be heated gently to a point just short of boiling for several hours daily for one week. It is a depressingly onerous undertaking.

Herbal Incense

One of the nicest ways to enjoy essential oils is to burn them! Making one's own incense is very satisfying, and is received with great delight as a present. It does need to be made well in advance of use. Ideally, make it up in the summer and keep in stone jars to blend and mature in a cool dark cupboard for a few months, giving the oils and spices a chance to combine and work upon each other. Here are two recipes:

ROSE AND SANDALWOOD INCENSE

1 oz. powdered gum benzoin
1 oz. powdered orris root
1 oz. ground lavender (well crushed with a pestle and mortar)
1 oz. ground cinnamon (also well crushed)
1 oz. ground rose petals (also well crushed)
1 teaspoon oil of lemon verbena
1 teaspoon oil of patchouli
1 teaspoon oil of rose
½ oz. sandalwood raspings

Mix very thoroughly – dry ingredients first, then adding gradually the mixed oils. Store before using – it improves with keeping.

VICTORIAN INCENSE

4 oz. damask roses crushed with pestle and mortar
2 oz. orris root
⅓ cup of rose water
2 oz. gum benzoin, powdered
5 drops oil of musk

Mix the orris root with the rose water, and add to the roses and gum benzoin. Add the oil, and mix all well.

Burning perfumes

The following delightfully scented incense mixture is for heating in a metal dish on the top of a radiator – it should not be ignited. The heat will release a pervasive but quite light delicate aroma.

3 oz. lavender flowers
3 oz. cloves
3 oz. cinnamon
4 oz. orris root
4 oz. gum benzoin
½ oz. of oils of sweet orange, clove, bergamot and rose mixed together

Add oils to the other ingredients and mix to a point when all the oil has been well absorbed. Store for a time before using.

Mixtures of herbs such as rosemary, southernwood and thyme can be burned in a little metal incense burner in a sickroom to give a most refreshing scent. Lavender or sage or mint added will give a stronger scent, and a few drops of any flower oil that is liked can be added one drop at a time while the mixture is burning. The herbs are, incidentally, disinfecting as they burn.

Another way of burning fragrant oils in a room is to cut a ring of asbestos (which can be bought in a small sheet from a builders' merchant) to fit around the top of the electric light bulb of a table lamp. A drop or two of oil placed on the ring will release its aroma when the bulb becomes hot; you can vary it from a scarcely discernible hint of perfume with just one drop, to a strength which does much to combat the accumulation of smoke and stuffiness at an overcrowded party. It is fun to try different combinations of scents on the ring, – two or three can be blended most effectively.

Do keep the twigs and stems that you clear from your

lemon verbena and other leaves when you are making pot-pourri; these, and especially the stems of lavender after they have been stripped, smell delicious on the fire; the combination of burning logs, lavender stems and perhaps a sprig of rosemary is a lovely antidote to stress!

One last thing I would like to suggest as a use for these delicious oils. Collect fir cones in the autumn and dry them very thoroughly. Blend two or three oils together in a small glass or jar, making sure that one of them has a fixative quality (such as musk, patchouli, sandalwood, vetiver, orange or lemon); possibilities are rose with orange and musk; carnation with clove and orange; wallflower and sandalwood. Blend these and others you want to try by mixing them a drop at a time on a little strip of blotting paper. Having decided on your blend, borrow a fairly thick brush from someone's paint box and paint each fir cone with the oil, as thinly as you can but getting the brush well into the cone where possible. Leave them to dry; if you have a box of pot-pourri as described in Chapter 7 you could spread your drying fircones in it which will add to their fragrance. When they are quite dry and there is no oiliness to be felt, tie a ribbon around them with a 6″ loop, – moss green or poppy red looks good for Christmas; these can be given from the Christmas tree, or to guests at a party; they do not need to be wrapped, and can be used as decoration until they are presented. Hung in the wardrobe, or on the wall above a radiator, their perfume will last at least until the following Christmas.

This is something to remember; herbs, or pot-pourri, in a warm place will be more generous with their scent, and they respond to a little care and interest. Turn the pot-pourri in your bowl, with your bare hand, from time to time; press sachets or sweet-bags, – just moving a herb-sack or a filled pomander will provoke a little waft of scent. Do not fill a china pomander too full; if it is packed tightly with herbs it will hardly smell at all – there needs to be room to shake them gently occasionally. As you experiment with herbs in all sorts of ways you will discover many more of their characteristics and endearing peculiarities, – not least their amazing versatility.

It has been possible only to touch very fleetingly on some of the many aspects of using and enjoying herbs, in the hope that some of the ideas outlined will start trains of thought leading to more ideas. There are a great number of interesting and informative books written by experts in their various fields, and a very few of these I have listed in a brief bibliography.

Suppliers

In Great Britain

Robert Jackson & Co. Ltd, 172 Piccadilly, W1 and 6a–6b Sloane Street, London SW1.
Essential oils, herbs and spices by the ounce, pot-pourri ingredients and pot-pourri kits. Herb pillows and all herb products. (Mail order catalogue available.)

G. Baldwin & Co., 173 Walworth Road, London SE17 1RW.
Essential oils, herbs and spices. List available. Mail order.

Culpeper Ltd, 21 Bruton Street, London W1X 7DA and 14 Bridewell Alley, Norwich, Norfolk.
Herbs, spices, pot-pourri, etc. Mail order catalogue from Hadstock Road, Cambridge.

Candlemakers Supplies, 4 Beaconsfield Terrace Road, London W14 0PP.
List. Mail order and booklet.

The Handicraft Shop, 83 Northgate, Canterbury, Kent.
Toy patterns and materials. Stuffings. Needlework. Catalogue. Mail order.

Chiltern Herb Farms Ltd, Buckland Common, Tring, Herts.
Herbs, herb teas and herb products.

The Bombay Emporium, 70 Grafton Way, London W1.
Full range of spices.

The Globe Galleries, Andover, Hants.
For containers of all sorts.

In Australia

Melody Farm Nursery, 616 Old Northern Road, Dural. N.S.W. 2158.
Hemphills Herbs and Spices Ltd, 745 Old Northern Road, Dural. N.S.W. 2158.
Beaufort Herb Farm, PO. Box 90, Cootamundra. N.S.W. 2590.
Mitchell Lilydale Herb Farm, Mangans Road, Lilydale. Victoria 3140.
Warrandyte Herbs, Huncy Road, Palmwoods. Qld 4555.
Hygienic Products, 104 Bowden Street, West Ryde. N.S.W. 2114.
Newton's Pharmacy, 323 Pitt Street, Sydney. N.S.W. 2000.
Calorie Control Pty Ltd, 55 Benaroon Road, Belfield. N.S.W. 2191.
Ralph Short Pty Ltd, 112 Durham Street, Hurstville. N.S.W. 2220.
Triad Health Products Pty Ltd, P.O. Box 31, Asquith. N.S.W. 2078.
Culpepers, 23 Phillimore Street, Fremantle. W.A.
Lassocks Garden Centre, 334 Henley Beach Road, Locksleys. S.A.

In South Africa

Healthy Life, 10 Murchies Passage, West Street, Durban 4001.

Attwells Health Foods Ltd, 6 African Life Arcade, West Street, Durban 4001.

Sunshine Health Centre, 84 Long Street, Cape Town 8001.

Reform Health and Beauty, 287 Long Street, Cape Town 8001.

Natural Remedies Centre and Health Food Shop, P.O. Box 5502, 2000 Johannesberg.

F. Kirchoff and Co. Ltd, P.O. Box 7756, 2000 Johannesberg.

Natural Medicinal Services Ltd, P.O. Box 4696, 2000 Johannesberg.

Natural Homoeopathic Laboratory, 1221 Zanza Building, 16 Proes Street, 0002 Pretoria.

Bibliography

Herbs for Health and Cookery, Claire Loewenfeld and Philippa Back (Pan Books)

Spices, Salt and Aromatics in the English Kitchen, Elizabeth David (Penguin)

Pot-pourris and Other Fragrant Delights, Jacqueline Heriteau (Lutterworth Press)

Rose Recipes from Olden Times, Eleanour Sinclair Rohde (Dover Books)

Herbs, Spices and Flavourings, Tom Stobart (David and Charles)

The Illustrated Herbal Handbook, Juliette de Bairacli Levy (Faber)

Out of print but can be found second-hand:

Herbal Delights, Mrs C. F. Leyel (Faber)

The Magic of Herbs, Mrs C. F. Leyel (Jonathan Cape)

A Book of Herbs, Dawn Macleod (Duckworth)

A Garden of Herbs, Eleanour Sinclair Rohde (Lee Warner)

Old Stillroom Book sources:

The Toilet of Flora (1775)

The Receipt Book of Charles Carter, cook to the Duke of Argyll (1732)
Mary Doggett, Her Book of Receipts (1682)
The Receipt Book of John Nott, cook to the Duke of Bolton (1723)
Delights for Ladies, Sir Hugh Platt (1659)
The Receipt Book of Elizabeth Cleland (1759)

Index